The Swallowtail
Butterfly

This book has been reviewed
for accuracy by
Walter L. Gojmerac
Professor of Entomology
University of Wisconsin—Madison.

Library of Congress Cataloging in Publication Data

Oda, Hidetomo.
   The swallowtail butterfly.

   (Nature close-ups)
   Translation of: Agehachō / text by Hidetomo Oda,
photographs by Hidekazu Kubo.
   Summary: Discusses the life cycle, behavior patterns,
and habitats of the swallowtail butterfly.
   1. Papilionidae—Juvenile literature. [1. Swallowtail butterflies. 2. Butterflies] I. Kubo, Hidekazu,
ill. II. Title. III. Series.
QL561.P203313   1986   595.78'9   85-28229

ISBN 0-8172-2542-0 (lib. bdg.)
ISBN 0-8172-2567-6 (softcover)

This edition first published in 1986 by Raintree Publishers Inc.

Text copyright © 1986 by Raintree Publishers Inc., translated from
Swallowtail copyright © 1979 by Jun Nanao and Hidetomo Oda.

Photographs copyright © 1979 by Hidekazu Kubo.

World English translation rights for Color Photo Books on Nature
arranged with Kaisei-Sha through Japan Foreign-Rights Center.

   3 4 5 6 7 8 9 0   90 89 88

The Swallowtail Butterfly

Raintree Publishers
Milwaukee

◀ A swallowtail on a cluster of amaryllis.

After fluttering from flower to flower, the butterfly lands on a particular blossom. It stretches its long, tube-like mouth, or proboscis, and uses it like a straw to drink flower nectar.

▶ A swallowtail in flight.

Some swallowtails have wingspreads measuring four to five inches. The giant swallowtail and the tiger swallowtail are the largest butterflies in North America.

Butterflies are beautiful to watch as they flutter gracefully from flower to flower, their brightly colored wings flashing in the sunlight. There are more than twenty-four thousand kinds, or species, of butterflies in the world. Scientists identify each species by its particular wing markings and colors.

Of all the butterflies in the world, the swallowtail is the only kind which has hind wings with curved tips. When it is in flight, its wings look like the long, tapering wings of the swallow. That is why it is called a swallowtail butterfly. There are many different kinds of swallowtails. They are among the largest and prettiest of the butterflies.

◀ **A female swallowtail laying her eggs.**

Many species of butterflies lay eggs only on certain kinds of plants, which they recognize by the odor of the plant and the shape of its leaves. The eggs are laid on the undersides of leaves, hidden from other insects and birds.

▶ **Swallowtail eggs laid on prickly ash leaves.**

The tiny egg is attached to the back of the leaf with a sticky mucous substance. When the egg is first laid, it is pale yellow and shines like a pearl.

The swallowtail has not always had such gorgeous wings. It was once a funny looking caterpillar. Like other butterflies, the swallowtail has four different stages in its life cycle. This series of changes is called a metamorphosis and includes: the egg, the larva, the pupa, and the adult.

After a male and female butterfly mate, the female finds a place to lay her eggs. She searches for a plant that will have the right kind of food for her offspring. Then she begins to lay her eggs, depositing them on the undersides of leaves. A female swallowtail may lay up to four or five batches of eggs in a season, up to one hundred eggs in all.

● **Plants of the Rutaceae family on which swallowtails lay their eggs.**

▲ Trifoliate orange   ▲ Prickly ash   ▲ Tangerine

◀ **A larva's head inside the egg.**

As it develops inside the egg, the larva's color changes from pale yellow to a reddish color. Also, its shell becomes darker.

▶ **The caterpillar emerges.**

The larva bites through the eggshell and crawls out onto the underside of the leaf. It attaches itself to the slippery leaf with silk threads, which it makes with its mouth.

Inside the egg, the swallowtail caterpillar, or larva, begins to develop. The number of days it takes for the egg to hatch depends on the weather. In summer it takes about four days. In early spring or late fall, it takes several days longer.

The swallowtail larva comes out of, emerges from, the egg by chewing a hole in the soft shell. The tiny, worm-like larva has a long segmented body covered with bristles. With its many legs, it is able to crawl easily on plant leaves.

▶ **A larva rests after emerging.**

After the larva emerges, it rests. Then it begins its first meal, eating the empty eggshell which is rich in food value.

◀ **A larva eating its eggshell.**

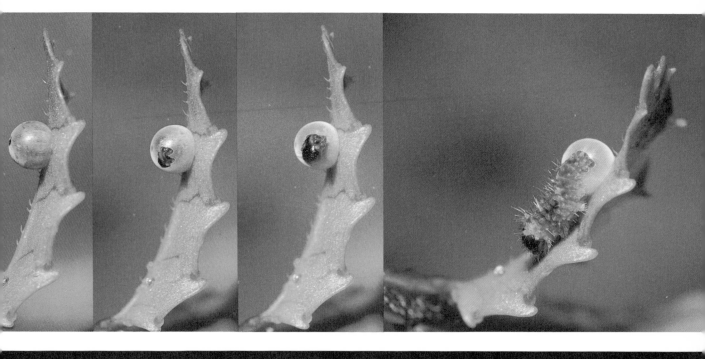

◄ A larva eating leaves.

The larva of this type of swallow-tail eats only the leaves of plants in the citrus family. Its many pairs of legs, with tiny hooks at the tips, enable the caterpillar to easily crawl about on the leaves.

► A larva after its first molt.

About three days after emerging, the larva outgrows its old skin and sheds it. The caterpillar has doubled in size by the time it molts the first time. Its color also changes with the first molt.

The caterpillar's purpose in life is to eat and grow. At first, the larva can only chew tiny holes in the plant leaves. But its jaws get stronger and soon it can eat entire leaves. By the time it is ready to enter the next stage of its life cycle, the larva may have grown to eight times its original size. The larva's body grows quickly, but its skin does not grow with it. So the larva sheds its old skin, or molts. The larva molts four times. Each new skin gives the fast-growing larva more room in which to grow.

▲ A young cricket, called a nymph.   ▲ Praying mantis nymphs.

● Some immature insects resemble their parents.

Unlike the swallowtail butterfly, crickets and praying mantises are not caterpillars during this stage of their development. Instead, these young insects look very much like their parents.

▲ Caterpillar before molting.

▲ Caterpillar after first molt.

▲ Caterpillar after second mol

◀ **Larvae in various instars.**

The larva eats constantly and out-grows its old skin. So it molts. The old skin splits open and the larva squirms out of it. With each molt, the larva's head grows wider and its body becomes longer.

▶ **A caterpillar in the fourth instar.**

This caterpillar has molted three times, and it has grown large and plump. The black and white colors act as camouflage to protect the cater-pillar from its enemies.

Scientists call the different stages of growth in the swallowtail larva's life instars. As soon as the caterpillar emerges from the egg, it is in its first instar. After the larva molts for the first time, it is in its second instar.

The larva changes color and looks stranger with each molt. Its skin turns a brownish-black and becomes mottled with white markings. From a distance, the caterpillar looks like bird droppings. This coloring pro-tects the larva from most birds and other enemies.

◀ **A caterpillar in the fourth instar.**

The larva has a large appetite in all stages of its development. A hungry caterpillar will strip all the leaves off a plant in its search for food.

▶ **A cricket molting.**

Many kinds of insects molt during the second stage of their development.

◀ **A larva in the fourth instar.**

This larva is preparing for its fourth and final molt. With front legs lifted and body slightly curved, it enters a brief sleeping period.

▶ **A green caterpillar emerging.**

As it molts, the larva casts off the old skin by stretching, then shrinking its body many times. The bright green caterpillar that emerges is in its fifth and final instar.

About five or six days after its third molt, the caterpillar gets ready to enter its most unusual and final instar. It stops eating. Then it lifts its front legs and curves the front part of its body upward. It rests in this position for about a day.

After a while, the fourth and last molt begins. The larva's old, stretched skin splits open behind its head, and the green head of the caterpillar in the fifth instar appears. First stretching, then shrinking its body, the caterpillar slowly sheds its old skin.

In the fifth instar, the larva's appearance is remarkably changed. The green caterpillar that emerges is very different from any of its former instars.

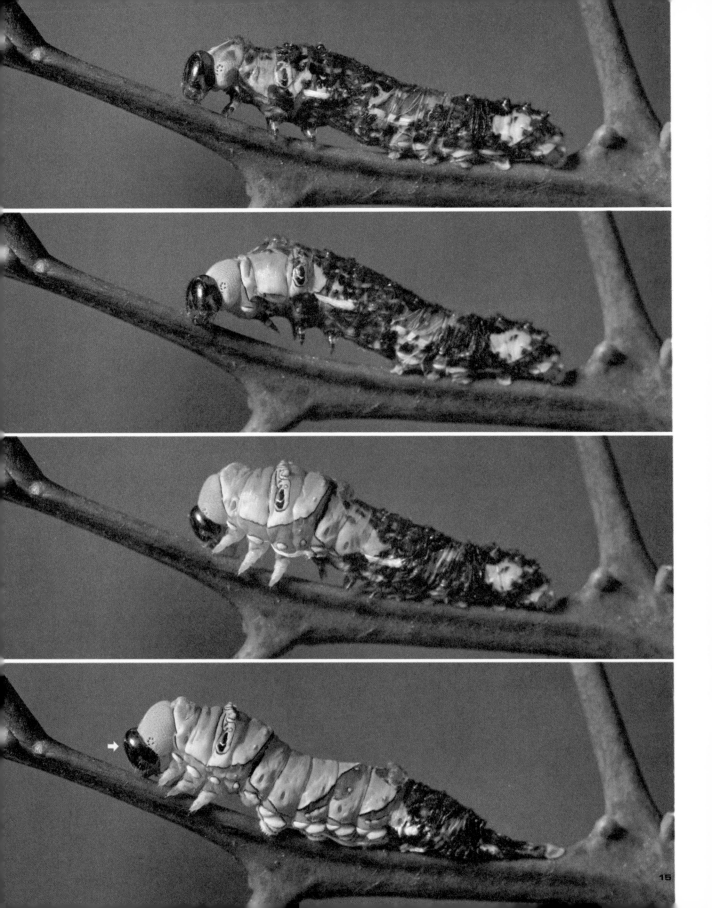

◄ A larva has shed its skin.

The fifth instar caterpillar is in its slightly curved upright position as it rests after molting. Behind it on the branch is its discarded skin.

► A caterpillar eating its skin.

Using its front legs and large chin, the swallowtail larva feeds itself. Its strong jaws chew up the discarded skin each time it molts.

After shedding its skin, the fifth instar caterpillar rests while it waits for its wet body to dry. At first, the bright green larva is full of wrinkles. Its new skin is a little too large. But soon, the caterpillar will grow big and fat, and the wrinkles will disappear.

After its body is dried, the caterpillar turns around on the branch and begins to eat the old skin. Each time it molts, the swallowtail caterpillar eats the skin it has shed. The old skin, rich in nutrients, provides nourishment for the ever-growing larva.

● An adult swallowtail butterfly.

The head of the swallowtail larva does not look at all like the head of the adult swallowtail butterfly.

▲ The adult swallowtail butterfly sucking nectar from a flower.

◄ A larva hides among the leaves.

The fifth instar swallowtail is hidden from its enemies by its green patterned body which blends with the vegetation on which it feeds.

► The caterpillar extends its horn.

When frightened, the swallowtail caterpillar extends its bright orange horn which emits a foul odor that discourages attackers.

The fifth instar larva has many ways of defending itself. With its bright green coloring, it blends in well with leafy vegetation, helping it to hide from natural hunters, or predators. Many species of swallowtails also have black or yellow markings. When the larva is in danger, it swells its body. The markings then look like large eyes, which may frighten the predator away. But its most unusual protective feature is its forked horn. The horn is usually pulled inside its body. But when the larva feels threatened, it extends its horn, which releases an unpleasant odor that discourages attackers.

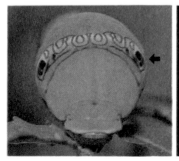

▲ Fake eyes

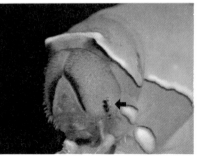

▲ Real eyes

● Two kinds of eyes.

The swallowtail's own eyes are not large, but it has false eyespots that frighten predators. The larva cannot see objects with its real eyes. It can only distinguish light from dark.

◀ **The caterpillar is resting.**

The fifth instar caterpillar rests as it prepares to become a pupa, the next stage in its life cycle.

▼ **The watery waste of a fifth instar caterpillar.**

A fifth instar caterpillar spends most of its time eating, just as it did during previous instars. The bright green larva has a huge appetite and continues to grow rapidly.

But five or six days after its fourth molt, the larva suddenly stops eating. It begins to prepare itself for the next stage in its development, when it becomes a pupa. It rests for a day. Then it becomes active again and excretes watery waste material. And it begins to crawl around, looking for a good place to pupate.

▶ **A caterpillar searching for a place to pupate.**

This swallowtail caterpillar has come out of its resting state and is now searching for a place where it can pupate.

◀ **The normal waste material from a caterpillar is round and solid.**

▲ The larva makes a foothold.

Facing downward, the caterpillar spins silk threads with its mouth and begins to make a foothold for itself.

▲ The larva repositions itself.

After it has spun its foothold, the larva turns around on the branch and begins to spin threads that will hold its upper body firmly in place.

When it finds a branch or twig it likes, the larva swings its head from side to side as it spins thread from its mouth and makes a tiny silk platform for itself. When this foothold is completed, the caterpillar turns around on the branch. It grips the foothold tightly with the tiny hooks on its hind legs.

Then the larva leans backward and swings its head, spinning white silk thread that goes around the upper part of its body, holding it to the branch.

As it waits for new changes to take place in its body, the caterpillar remains attached to the branch, even in high winds and stormy weather.

▼ **A caterpillar spinning silk.** The caterpillar swings its head back and forth as it spins the silk thread that connects its upper body to the tree. As it spins, it holds the thread in position with its front legs.

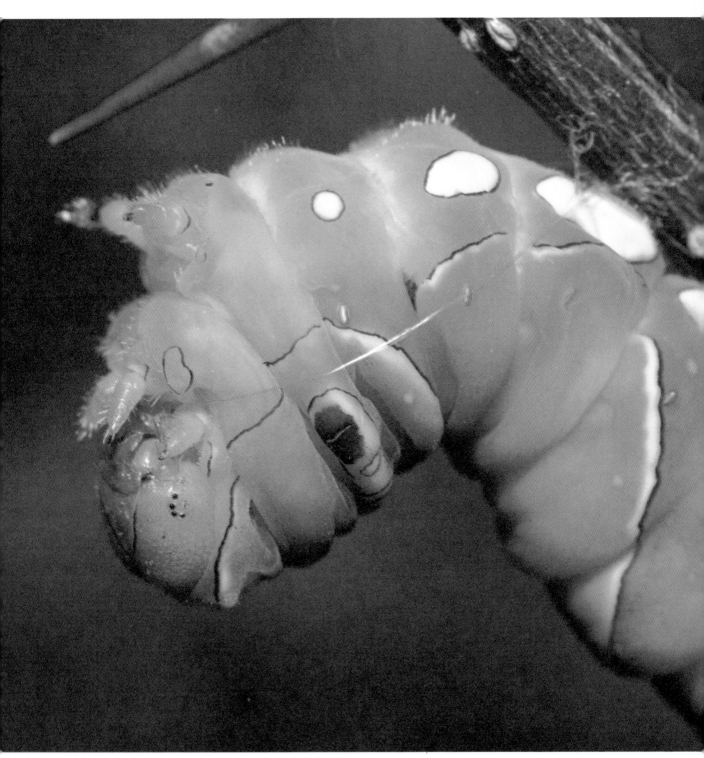

▲ **The larva finishes spinning its silk.**

When the caterpillar has spun the last of its silk threads, it passes its body through the loop of thread, attaching itself to the branch.

▲ **The larva is anchored to the branch.**

The caterpillar's work is completed. Now it stays still and waits during the prepupal stage, which usually lasts about a day.

After it has spun its last silk threads, the caterpillar remains suspended and motionless. This prepupal stage is the most dangerous time for the swallowtail. While it is hanging this way, it is helpless. The larva cannot defend itself in any way. It may be eaten by birds, toads, or other animals.

Other insects may harm the swallowtail larva, too. Certain kinds of wasps lay their eggs on the caterpillar during its prepupal stage. When the eggs hatch, the wasp larvae burrow into the body of the caterpillar and begin to feed on it. Gradually, the caterpillar weakens and dies.

▼ **A small wasp laying eggs on the prepupal swallowtail.**

Certain kinds of wasps lay eggs on the caterpillar's body. After the eggs hatch, the wasp larvae burrow inside and begin to feed on the helpless swallowtail.

The prepupal stage is not a long one, and the larva's skin soon begins to turn white and dry up. Within a day after the caterpillar has spun the last of its silk thread, it sheds its skin for the last time. When the old skin is discarded, the wrinkled chrysalis emerges. The

◀A caterpillar resting in its prepupal stage.

chrysalis forms a protective covering for the pupa. During this third
stage of the butterfly's life cycle,
nothing seems to be happening.
But actually, mysterious changes
are taking place. The body of the
adult butterfly is forming.

● **The larva becomes a pupa.**

During this stage of the swallowtail's
life cycle, it changes from a caterpillar into a pupa with a protective
covering, or chrysalis. The silk
threads bind the chrysalis securely to
this tree branch.

◄ Protective coloring of the chrysalis.

The protective coloring of the chrysalis helps it blend in with its surroundings, keeping it hidden from natural predators.

▶ The developing butterfly becomes visible.

Inside the chrysalis, the body organs of the butterfly are developing and the wings are slowly forming.

◄ The pupa enclosed in its green chrysalis.

Even in the pupal stage, the butterfly may fall victim to preying insects.

The amount of time the swallowtail spends in the pupal, or resting, stage depends on the species of butterfly and on the weather. If the caterpillar enters the pupal stage in late fall, it will hibernate all winter. In the summer, the butterfly may take only ten or fifteen days to develop inside the chrysalis.

The swallowtail chrysalis is usually green in summer and brown in winter. In either case, the coloring blends in with the leaves and branches and helps protect the developing butterfly.

● Incomplete metamorphosis.

Some insects, like grasshoppers, don't have a pupal stage. When they shed their skin as nymphs they look just like winged adults. Their development is called an incomplete metamorphosis.

▲ The cricket nymph sheds its skin and becomes an adult with wings.

▲ **A swallowtail emerges.** First, the chrysalis splits open. Then the swallowtail slowly emerges. It clings to a branch as its wet, wrinkled wings dry out and expand.

Changes have now taken place inside the chrysalis. The fat body of the caterpillar has turned into the slender, streamlined body of the adult butterfly.

When the time is right, the shell of the chrysalis turns white and becomes transparent. It splits behind the head of the butterfly, which slowly emerges. First the legs, then its antennae appear. After it has climbed completely out of its shell, the butterfly crawls onto a branch and waits for its wings to dry. The swallowtail hangs upside down so its wings can stretch out and dry. This takes about an hour.

The beautiful, fragile wings are perfect, with each scale in place. They will carry the swallowtail gracefully through the final stage of its life. As an adult, it will find a mate and, in a few short weeks, will begin to lay eggs. And the fascinating life cycle of the swallowtail will begin again for a new generation of butterflies.

▶ **An adult swallowtail fully emerged from its chrysalis.** If the butterfly falls off the branch before its wings are dry, they will remain stiff and wrinkled and it will be unable to fly.

GLOSSARY

camouflage—to hide by blending with the environment. (p. 13)

chrysalis—a protective covering formed by butterflies in their pupal stage of development. (pp. 26, 27, 29)

instars—the different stages of growth in the swallowtail's life. With each molt, the swallowtail enters a new instar. (pp. 13, 14, 17)

metamorphosis—a process of development during which physical changes take place. Complete metamorphosis involves four stages: egg, larva, pupa, and adult. Incomplete metamorphosis occurs in three stages: egg, nymph, and adult. (pp. 7, 29)

molt—to shed the outer skin. (pp. 10, 13, 14)

nymph—the second stage in the life cycle of those insects that go through three stages of development: egg, nymph, and adult. (pp. 10, 29)

predator—an animal that hunts or kills other animals for food. (pp. 18, 29)

proboscis—a tube-like mouth which is used for sucking liquids. (p. 4)

pupate—to become a pupa. (p. 20)

species—a group of animals which scientists have identified as having common traits. (p. 4)